Time in The Word

ECCLESIASTES
Series 21 of 66

Paula Nafziger

Large Print—18 point

King James Today

Title .... Time in The Word ECCLESIASTES
Subtitle .... Large Print—18 point, King James Today
Series .... 21 of 66
AU Prepared for Publication ...... Paula Nafziger, Chaplain
ISBN-13 978-1-948136-73-0

Scripture is from an easier-to-read King James Version, King James Today™
©2019 Paula Nafziger, All rights reserved   9 8 7 6 5 4 3 2 1

Other books available for purchase: **Books of the Bible** in multiple formats:
• Enhanced 13, Large 18, Giant 24, and Super Giant 28 point type (font size)

Left Notetaker Lines   Right Notetaker Lines   Notetaker Margins   Triple Notetaker Margins

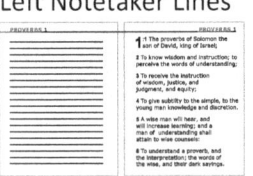 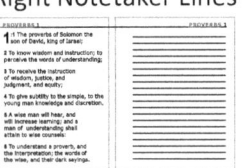 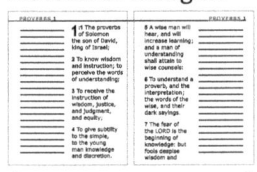

Fool-Proof Wisdom, Proverbs 1 Have you ever wanted to slow down and study just one book or chapter of the Bible at a time? This detailed verse-by-verse study will help you think as you read in ways that cause you to retain God's word in your heart. Get ready to study hard and come away not only knowing what the verses mean but enjoy the learning process. The variety of vocabulary activities capture your attention as they teach. Before you realize it, you'll know an entire chapter and will be able to recite all or most of it with little effort. Begin this first in the series of all 31 chapters of Proverbs. • Designed to keep your mind engaged in active learning • Includes self-tests, fill-in, true/false, yes/no and recall • Easier–to–read King James Version

Grow Time WORD Journals encourage you to read with a plan, write a verse you find interesting, pay attention to details you choose to research, then formulate personal application.
• **Grow Time 365** The Bible   • **Grow Time 187** Law/Torah   • **Grow Time 87** Paul's Letters
• **Grow Time 364** Old Testament   • **Grow Time 183** Major Prophets • **Grow Time 67** Minor Prophets
• **Grow Time 260** New Testament   • **Grow Time 180** WORD Journal   • **Grow Time 56** Letters & Prophecy
• **Grow Time 249** Historical Books • **Grow Time 150** Psalms   • **Grow Time 31** Proverbs
• **Grow Time 243** Poetry/Wisdom   • **Grow Time 117** Gospels & Acts • **Grow Time 12** 12 Months in Proverbs

PROVERBIOS en Español, **PROVERBS** in English
Letra Grande—18 puntos Reina Valera 1909, Large Print—18 point King James Today

PROVERBS Writing God's Word This book will help you focus on the meaning and implications of God's message, notice details you may have overlooked, and better comprehend the book of Proverbs. Writing God's word by hand causes you to slow down as you read giving you time to ponder, meditate, or converse with yourself on each word and verse. Your knowledge and understanding will increase as you write. With suggestions on how you can use this book, you'll hand copy the book of Proverbs at a do-what-works-for-you pace. Features include: • Easier-to-read King James • LARGE print—18-20 point type • Lined pages ready for you to write

Read, Write & REAP ECCLESIASTES will keep you busy in the Bible encouraging spiritual growth, intelligent conversation, and friendly fellowship. It's ideal for personal, student, or group study. The text is formatted so you can read and re-write it line-by-line in your preferred style. At the back of the book you'll find the REAP Bible Study System to: **R**ead the chapter, choose a verse or two hand copy and re-write from a different translation, **E**xamine the text using your favorite resources, **A**cknowledge what God prompts your heart to act upon, attest to personal experiences, then "talk to God" in written **P**rayer. Includes: • Easier–to-read King James Version • LARGE print 18-20 point type • REAP Bible Study System

Time in The Word – ECCLESIASTES

King James Today 4
Bookmarker 7
Introduction 8
Writing Ideas 10
Bible Verse Art 13
Ecclesiastes 1 79
Ecclesiastes 2 37
Ecclesiastes 3 59
Ecclesiastes 4 79
Ecclesiastes 5 95
Ecclesiastes 6 111
Ecclesiastes 7 123
Ecclesiastes 8 143
Ecclesiastes 9 159
Ecclesiastes 10 175
Ecclesiastes 11 191
Ecclesiastes 12 203

N.T. Key: Direct speaking of Christ appears in *italics*. Quotation of direct words of God or Christ made by Their messengers, or from the Old Testament, appears in *italic underlined*. The Bible in its entirety is the Word of God.

KING JAMES TODAY™

What makes this contemporary King James Version easier-to-read?

• Unnecessary word endings "est, eth, st, th, and ith" are dropped, **e.g.**, build<u>est</u> (build), build<u>eth</u> (builds), do<u>st</u> (do), lie<u>th</u> (lie), sa<u>ith</u> (says).

• Old English is replaced **e.g.**, art (are), hither (here), nigh (near), oft (often), thee (you), thine (your), thou (you), thy (you) thyself (yourself), unto (to), wast (were), ye (you).

• Old English spelling is updated **e.g.**, labour (labor), licence (license), musick (music), publick (public), shew (show), wilt (will).

• Ye, you, you-ward, your, yours, and yourselves, referring to more than one person, is noted by a superscript P (for plural) **e.g.**, you^p.

• Spelling consistency for proper nouns **e.g.**, Balac (Balak), Elias (Elijah), Esaias (Isaiah), Jonas (Jonah), Noe (Noah), Osee (Hosea), Sion (Zion), Timotheus (Timothy).

Comparison of scripture:
King **J**ames **V**ersion versus **K**ing **J**ames **T**oday:

> What profit hath a man of all his labour which he taketh under the sun? **Ecclesiastes 1:3 KJV**

> What profit has a man of all his labor which he takes under the sun? **Ecclesiastes 1:3 KJT**

Let us hear the conclusion of the whole matter:
Fear God, and keep his commandments:
for this is the whole duty of man.
For God shall bring every work into
judgment, with every secret thing,
whether it be good, or whether it be evil.

Ecclesiastes 12:13-14

Let us hear the conclusion
of the whole matter:
Fear God,
and keep his commandments:
for this is the whole duty of man.
For God shall bring every work
into judgment,
with every secret thing,
whether it be good,
or whether it be evil.

Ecclesiastes 12:13-14

Introduction

Time in the Word offers a variety of ideas to keep you *busy in the Bible*™ as you read, write, study and note what you learn in church, at home, or wherever your journey takes you.

This workbook includes God's word to read on your own or follow along with your ministry leader.

A blank line follows every line of text to give you room to write each verse by hand. You'll choose a style that fits your interest: Copy It, Define It, Personalize It, or Compare It *(see examples on the pages that follow)*.

Writing scripture by hand causes you to slow down as you read giving you time to focus on the meaning and implications of God's message, notice details you may have overlooked, and comprehend the word, verse, chapter, and book. Your knowledge, recall, and understanding of God's word will increase just by writing it out.

When the Israelites were about to enter the promised land, God described what a wise king would do:

> 18 **And it shall be, when he sits upon the throne of his kingdom, that he shall write him a copy of this law in a book out of that which is before the priests the Levites:** 19 **And it shall be with him, and he shall read therein all the days**

***of his life: that he may learn to fear the Lord his God, to keep all the words of this law and these statutes, to do them:** 20 **That his heart be not lifted up above his brethren, and that he turn not aside from the commandment, to the right hand, or to the left: to the end that he may prolong his days in his kingdom, he, and his children, in the midst of Israel.** Deuteronomy 17:18-20*

If you are in a position to influence others, just as a king, you are a leader. As a leader it would be wise to practice the same spiritual discipline—write a copy of God's word, have it nearby, read it "all the days of our life", learn to fear, honor, and respect God, keep His laws and statutes by doing them, and remain a humble servant devoted to God, His word, and His people.

This book is ideal for sermon notetakers, personal, student or group Bible study, transitional readers, and the visually impaired. It includes:

- Bible Art pages to draw your favorite verse
- Blank lines/wide margins for sermon & study notes
- Coloring pages for calm, relaxing, stress relief
- Easier-to-read King James Version in LARGE print

Writing Ideas

Copy It method: Copy the verses by hand exactly as written onto the lines provided. This simple method will help you keep focused on the verse without distraction.

Define It method: Use Bible study tools such as a concordance, cross-references, a regular or Bible dictionary, lexicon, or study Bible to increase your understanding of the words used in the verse. Be sure to keep the meaning within the context of the message.

Personalize It method: Make the scripture apply to you specifically by inserting your words, speaking style, understanding, thoughts and art or doodles. Again be careful to accurately describe what the author intended by making "context king" meaning you consider the words, phrases, and verses with their surrounding words, verses, paragraphs and circumstances.

Compare It method: Use a different translation of the Bible to write what it states word-for-word. It will help you see differences in ways to communicate God's word. Choose a translation compiled of Holy Spirit filled, biblically accurate scholars.

Ideally, it would be best to use one method per chapter, but you can choose to complete each page using a different method if that helps you keep engaged and learning. *Do what works for you!*

COPY IT

12 There is a way which seems right to a man,
There is a way which seems right to a man,

but the end thereof are the ways of death.
but the end thereof are the ways of death. **EXAMPLE**

☑ Copy KJT ☐ Definitions added ☐ KJT My Way ☐ Translation compared: _____

DEFINE IT

12 There is a way which seems right to a man,
There is a course of live/path that seems upright

but the end thereof are the ways of death.
to a person, but his future are the paths of ruin.

☐ Copy KJT ☑ Definitions added ☐ KJT My Way ☐ Translation compared: _____

PERSONALIZE IT

12 There is a way which seems right to a man,
There is a way that seems right to me (at the time),

but the end thereof are the ways of death.
but I'm ruining my future (stop using illegal drugs!)

☐ Copy KJT ☐ Definitions added ☑ KJT My Way ☐ Translation compared: _____

OR, COMPARE IT

12 There is a way which seems right to a man,
There is a way which seemeth right unto a man,

but the end thereof are the ways of death.
But the end thereof are the ways of death.

☐ Copy KJT ☐ Definitions added ☐ KJT My Way ☑ Translation compared: Tanakh

EXAMPLE

Bible Verse Art 1) Pick a verse from the chapter. 2) Sketch in the words you want to bring attention to first—leaving space to add the rest of the verse above, below or around it. 3) Use your imagination to make the verse visually expressive.

Bible Verse Art

One creative way to meditate on God's word is to choose a verse or portion of one to create visual art. You can create a poster, bookmarker, or draw directly in the margin of your Bible. Some people refer to this as "Bible Journaling," but traditionally journaling is the expression of thoughts on paper. To keep written journaling separate from art journaling, the phrase Bible Verse Art is used.

Supplies used for Bible Verse Art might include a pencil, eraser, pens, highlighters, watercolor pencils or paint, stamps, washi tape, or stickers. Following are helpful tips:

☞ Choose a verse or portion of one, then read it a few times. Think of what the verse means to you and how you might express the words in an art form. Studying about the verse will help your creativity flow from having a better understanding of its meaning and message.

☞ Determine which word or words communicate the main message, most important part of the verse, or ones that stand out to you for any reason.

☞ Use a pencil to sketch your design, leaving room for the remainder of the text and drawing. Use your eraser to adjust your art until you are happy with the results, then finalize it with darker lines, or by adding color.

☞ Add symbols, icons, logos, doodles, or any graphic you are inspired to trace or create. You don't need to be "artistic" to enjoy the freedom of being creative.

☞ You might want to sign and date your art then consider blessing someone with your creation.

Ecclesiastes 1

Bible Verse Art 1) Pick a verse from the chapter. 2) Sketch in the words you want to bring attention to first—leaving space to add the rest of the verse above, below or around it. 3) Use your imagination to make the verse visually expressive.

Notes on Ecclesiastes

Notes — Ecclesiastes 1

Ecclesiastes 1
King James Today

1:1 The words of the Preacher, the son of David, king in Jerusalem.

2 Vanity of vanities, says the Preacher, vanity of vanities; all is vanity.

3 What profit has a man of all his labor which he takes under the sun?

4 One generation passes away,

Ecclesiastes 1

and another generation comes:

but the earth abides for ever.

5 The sun also arises, and the

sun goes down, and hastes to

his place where he arose.

6 The wind goes toward the south,

and turns about to the north; it whirls

about continually, and the wind returns

again according to his circuits.

7 All the rivers run into the sea; yet the

sea is not full; to the place from whence

the rivers come, there they return again.

8 All things are full of labor; man cannot

utter it: the eye is not satisfied with

seeing, nor the ear filled with hearing.

9 The thing that has been, it is that

Ecclesiastes 1

which shall be; and that which is done

is that which shall be done: and there

is no new thing under the sun.

10 Is there any thing whereof it may

be said, See, this is new? it has been

already of old time, which was before us.

11 There is no remembrance of former

things; neither shall there be any

remembrance of things that are to

Ecclesiastes 1
King James Today

come with those that shall come after.

12 I the Preacher was king over Israel in Jerusalem.

13 And I gave my heart to seek and search out by wisdom concerning all things that are done under heaven: this sore travail has God given to the sons of man to be exercised therewith.

Ecclesiastes 1

14 I have seen all the works that are done under the sun; and, behold, all is vanity and vexation of spirit.

15 That which is crooked cannot be made straight: and that which is wanting cannot be numbered.

16 I communed with my own heart, saying, Lo, I am come to great estate, and have gotten more wisdom than

Ecclesiastes 1
King James Today

all they that have been before me in

Jerusalem: yea, my heart had great

experience of wisdom and knowledge.

17 And I gave my heart to know

wisdom, and to know madness

and folly: I perceived that this

also is vexation of spirit.

18 For in much wisdom is much

grief: and he that increases

Ecclesiastes 1

knowledge increases sorrow.

Notes — Ecclesiastes 1

Notes — Ecclesiastes 1

Notes — Ecclesiastes 1

Ecclesiastes 1

Doodles, Memory verse, Notes & Quotes

31

Ecclesiastes 2

Bible Verse Art 1) Pick a verse from the chapter. 2) Sketch in the words you want to bring attention to first—leaving space to add the rest of the verse above, below or around it. 3) Use your imagination to make the verse visually expressive.

Notes on Ecclesiastes

Notes — Ecclesiastes 2

Ecclesiastes 2
King James Today

2:1 I said in my heart, Go to now, I will prove you with mirth, therefore enjoy pleasure: and, behold, this also is vanity.

2 I said of laughter, It is mad: and of mirth, What does it?

3 I sought in my heart to give myself to wine, yet acquainting my heart with wisdom; and to lay hold on folly, till I might see what was that good for the

❏ Copy KJT or My Way ❏ Definitions added ❏ Translation compared: _____

Ecclesiastes 2

sons of men, which they should do under

the heaven all the days of their life.

4 I made me great works; I builded

me houses; I planted me vineyards:

5 I made me gardens and orchards, and I

planted trees in them of all kind of fruits:

6 I made me pools of water,

to water therewith the wood

that brings forth trees:

7 I got me servants and maidens,

and had servants born in my house;

also I had great possessions of

great and small cattle above all that

were in Jerusalem before me:

8 I gathered me also silver and gold,

and the peculiar treasure of kings

and of the provinces: I got me men

Ecclesiastes 2

singers and women singers, and the

delights of the sons of men, as musical

instruments, and that of all sorts.

9 So I was great, and increased

more than all that were before

me in Jerusalem: also my

wisdom remained with me.

10 And whatsoever my eyes desired

I kept not from them, I withheld not

Ecclesiastes 2
King James Today

my heart from any joy; for my heart

rejoiced in all my labor: and this

was my portion of all my labor.

11 Then I looked on all the works that

my hands had wrought, and on the labor

that I had labored to do: and, behold,

all was vanity and vexation of spirit,

and there was no profit under the sun.

12 And I turned myself to behold wisdom,

Ecclesiastes 2

and madness, and folly: for what can

the man do that comes after the king?

even that which has been already done.

13 Then I saw that wisdom excels

folly, as far as light excels darkness.

14 The wise man's eyes are in his

head; but the fool walks in darkness:

and I myself perceived also that

Ecclesiastes 2
King James Today

one event happens to them all.

15 Then said I in my heart, As it happens to the fool, so it happens even to me; and why was I then more wise? Then I said in my heart, that this also is vanity.

16 For there is no remembrance of the wise more than of the fool for ever; seeing that which now is in the days to come shall all be forgotten. And

Ecclesiastes 2

how dies the wise man? as the fool.

17 Therefore I hated life; because

the work that is wrought under

the sun is grievous to me: for all

is vanity and vexation of spirit.

18 Yea, I hated all my labor which I had

taken under the sun: because I should

leave it to the man that shall be after me.

19 And who knows whether he shall be a wise man or a fool? yet shall he have rule over all my labor wherein I have labored, and wherein I have showed myself wise under the sun. This is also vanity.

20 Therefore I went about to cause my heart to despair of all the labor which I took under the sun.

21 For there is a man whose labor is

Ecclesiastes 2

in wisdom, and in knowledge, and in

equity; yet to a man that has not labored

therein shall he leave it for his portion.

This also is vanity and a great evil.

22 For what has man of all his labor,

and of the vexation of his heart, wherein

he has labored under the sun?

23 For all his days are sorrows, and his

travail grief; yea, his heart takes not

Ecclesiastes 2

rest in the night. This is also vanity.

24 There is nothing better for a man, than that he should eat and drink, and that he should make his soul enjoy good in his labor. This also I saw, that it was from the hand of God.

25 For who can eat, or who else can hasten hereunto, more than I?

Ecclesiastes 2

26 For God gives to a man that is good in his sight wisdom, and knowledge, and joy: but to the sinner he gives travail, to gather and to heap up, that he may give to him that is good before God. This also is vanity and vexation of spirit.

Notes — Ecclesiastes 2

Notes — Ecclesiastes 2

Notes — Ecclesiastes 2

Ecclesiastes 2

Doodles, Memory verse, Notes & Quotes

53

Ecclesiastes 3

Bible Verse Art 1) Pick a verse from the chapter. 2) Sketch in the words you want to bring attention to first—leaving space to add the rest of the verse above, below or around it. 3) Use your imagination to make the verse visually expressive.

Notes on Ecclesiastes

Notes — Ecclesiastes 3

Ecclesiastes 3
King James Today

3:1 To every thing there is a season, and a time to every purpose under the heaven:

2 A time to be born, and a time to die; a time to plant, and a time to pluck up that which is planted;

3 A time to kill, and a time to heal; a time to break down,

❏ Copy KJT or My Way ❏ Definitions added ❏ Translation compared: _____

Ecclesiastes 3

and a time to build up;

4 A time to weep, and a time to laugh;

a time to mourn, and a time to dance;

5 A time to cast away stones, and

a time to gather stones together;

a time to embrace, and a time

to refrain from embracing;

Ecclesiastes 3
King James Today

6 A time to get, and a time to lose; a time to keep, and a time to cast away;

7 A time to rend, and a time to sew; a time to keep silence, and a time to speak;

8 A time to love, and a time to hate; a time of war, and a time of peace.

9 What profit has he that works

Ecclesiastes 3

in that wherein he labors?

10 I have seen the travail, which

God has given to the sons of

men to be exercised in it.

11 He has made every thing beautiful

in his time: also he has set the world

in their heart, so that no man can

find out the work that God makes

from the beginning to the end.

12 I know that there is no good in them, but for a man to rejoice, and to do good in his life.

13 And also that every man should eat and drink, and enjoy the good of all his labor, it is the gift of God.

14 I know that, whatsoever God does, it

Ecclesiastes 3

shall be for ever: nothing can be put to

it, nor any thing taken from it: and God

does it, that men should fear before him.

15 That which has been is now; and

that which is to be has already been;

and God requires that which is past.

16 And moreover I saw under the

sun the place of judgment, that

wickedness was there; and the place of

Ecclesiastes 3
King James Today

righteousness, that iniquity was there.

17 I said in my heart, God shall

judge the righteous and the wicked:

for there is a time there for every

purpose and for every work.

18 I said in my heart concerning the

estate of the sons of men, that God

might manifest them, and that they might

Ecclesiastes 3

see that they themselves are beasts.

19 For that which befalls the sons of men befalls beasts; even one thing befalls them: as the one dies, so dies the other; yea, they have all one breath; so that a man has no preeminence above a beast: for all is vanity.

20 All go to one place; all are of the

Ecclesiastes 3
King James Today

dust, and all turn to dust again.

21 Who knows the spirit of man that goes upward, and the spirit of the beast that goes downward to the earth?

22 Wherefore I perceive that there is nothing better, than that a man should rejoice in his own works; for that is his portion: for who shall bring

Ecclesiastes 3

him to see what shall be after him?

Notes — Ecclesiastes 3

Notes — Ecclesiastes 3

Notes — Ecclesiastes 3

Ecclesiastes 3

Doodles, Memory verse, Notes & Quotes

Ecclesiastes 4

Bible Verse Art 1) Pick a verse from the chapter. 2) Sketch in the words you want to bring attention to first—leaving space to add the rest of the verse above, below or around it. 3) Use your imagination to make the verse visually expressive.

Notes on Ecclesiastes

Notes — Ecclesiastes 4

Ecclesiastes 4
King James Today

4:1 So I returned, and considered all the oppressions that are done under the sun: and behold the tears of such as were oppressed, and they had no comforter; and on the side of their oppressors there was power; but they had no comforter.

2 Wherefore I praised the dead which are already dead more than

Ecclesiastes 4

the living which are yet alive.

3 Yea, better is he than both they, which has not yet been, who has not seen the evil work that is done under the sun.

4 Again, I considered all travail, and every right work, that for this a man is envied of his neighbor. This is also vanity and vexation of spirit.

5 The fool folds his hands together,

and eats his own flesh.

6 Better is a handful with quietness,

than both the hands full with

travail and vexation of spirit.

7 Then I returned, and I saw

vanity under the sun.

8 There is one alone, and there is not

Ecclesiastes 4

a second; yea, he has neither child nor

brother: yet is there no end of all his

labor; neither is his eye satisfied with

riches; neither says he, For whom do I

labor, and bereave my soul of good? This

is also vanity, yea, it is a sore travail.

9 Two are better than one; because they

have a good reward for their labor.

10 For if they fall, the one will lift

Ecclesiastes 4

up his fellow: but woe to him that

is alone when he falls; for he has

not another to help him up.

11 Again, if two lie together,

then they have heat: but how

can one be warm alone?

12 And if one prevail against him,

two shall withstand him; and a

Ecclesiastes 4

threefold cord is not quickly broken.

13 Better is a poor and a wise child

than an old and foolish king, who

will no more be admonished.

14 For out of prison he comes to

reign; whereas also he that is born

in his kingdom becomes poor.

15 I considered all the living which

Ecclesiastes 4

walk under the sun, with the second

child that shall stand up in his stead.

16 There is no end of all the people,

even of all that have been before

them: they also that come after shall

not rejoice in him. Surely this also

is vanity and vexation of spirit.

Notes — Ecclesiastes 4

Notes — Ecclesiastes 4

Ecclesiastes 4

Doodles, Memory verse, Notes & Quotes

Ecclesiastes 5

Bible Verse Art 1) Pick a verse from the chapter. 2) Sketch in the words you want to bring attention to first—leaving space to add the rest of the verse above, below or around it. 3) Use your imagination to make the verse visually expressive.

Notes on Ecclesiastes

Ecclesiastes 5

Ecclesiastes 5
King James Today

5:1 Keep your foot when you go to the house of God, and be more ready to hear, than to give the sacrifice of fools: for they consider not that they do evil.

2 Be not rash with your mouth, and let not your heart be hasty to utter any thing before God: for God is in heaven, and you upon earth: therefore let your words be few.

Ecclesiastes 5

3 For a dream comes through the multitude of business; and a fool's voice is known by multitude of words.

4 When you vow a vow to God, defer not to pay it; for he has no pleasure in fools: pay that which you have vowed.

5 Better is it that you should not vow, than that you should vow and not pay.

Ecclesiastes 5

6 Suffer not your mouth to cause your flesh to sin; neither say you before the angel, that it was an error: wherefore should God be angry at your voice, and destroy the work of your hands?

7 For in the multitude of dreams and many words there are also divers vanities: but fear you God.

8 If you see the oppression of the

Ecclesiastes 5

poor, and violent perverting of

judgment and justice in a province,

marvel not at the matter: for he that

is higher than the highest regards;

and there be higher than they.

9 Moreover the profit of the earth is for

all: the king himself is served by the field.

10 He that loves silver shall

not be satisfied with silver; nor

he that loves abundance with

increase: this is also vanity.

11 When goods increase, they are

increased that eat them: and what good

is there to the owners thereof, saving

the beholding of them with their eyes?

12 The sleep of a laboring man

is sweet, whether he eat little or

much: but the abundance of the

Ecclesiastes 5

rich will not suffer him to sleep.

13 There is a sore evil which I have

seen under the sun, namely, riches kept

for the owners thereof to their hurt.

14 But those riches perish by evil

travail: and he begets a son, and

there is nothing in his hand.

15 As he came forth of his mother's

womb, naked shall he return to go as he

came, and shall take nothing of his labor,

which he may carry away in his hand.

16 And this also is a sore evil,

that in all points as he came, so

shall he go: and what profit has he

that has labored for the wind?

17 All his days also he eats in

darkness, and he has much sorrow

Ecclesiastes 5

and wrath with his sickness.

18 Behold that which I have seen:

it is good and comely for one to eat

and to drink, and to enjoy the good

of all his labor that he takes under

the sun all the days of his life, which

God gives him: for it is his portion.

19 Every man also to whom God

has given riches and wealth, and has

given him power to eat thereof, and

to take his portion, and to rejoice in

his labor; this is the gift of God.

20 For he shall not much remember

the days of his life; because God

answers him in the joy of his heart.

Ecclesiastes 5

Doodles, Memory verse, Notes & Quotes

Ecclesiastes 6

Bible Verse Art 1) Pick a verse from the chapter. 2) Sketch in the words you want to bring attention to first—leaving space to add the rest of the verse above, below or around it. 3) Use your imagination to make the verse visually expressive.

Notes on Ecclesiastes

Ecclesiastes 6

Ecclesiastes 6
King James Today

6:1 There is an evil which I have seen under the sun, and it is common among men:

2 A man to whom God has given riches, wealth, and honor, so that he wants nothing for his soul of all that he desires, yet God gives him not power to eat thereof, but a stranger eats it: this is vanity, and it is an evil disease.

Ecclesiastes 6

3 If a man beget a hundred children,

and live many years, so that the

days of his years be many, and his

soul be not filled with good, and also

that he have no burial; I say, that an

untimely birth is better than he.

4 For he comes in with vanity, and

departs in darkness, and his name

shall be covered with darkness.

5 Moreover he has not seen the sun, nor known any thing: this has more rest than the other.

6 Yea, though he live a thousand years twice told, yet has he seen no good: do not all go to one place?

7 All the labor of man is for his mouth, and yet the appetite is not filled.

Ecclesiastes 6

8 For what has the wise more than the fool? what has the poor, that knows to walk before the living?

9 Better is the sight of the eyes than the wandering of the desire: this is also vanity and vexation of spirit.

10 That which has been is named already, and it is known that it is man: neither may he contend with

him that is mightier than he.

11 Seeing there be many things that increase vanity, what is man the better?

12 For who knows what is good for man in this life, all the days of his vain life which he spends as a shadow? for who can tell a man what shall be after him under the sun?

Ecclesiastes 6

Doodles, Memory verse, Notes & Quotes

Ecclesiastes 7

Bible Verse Art 1) Pick a verse from the chapter. 2) Sketch in the words you want to bring attention to first—leaving space to add the rest of the verse above, below or around it. 3) Use your imagination to make the verse visually expressive.

Notes on Ecclesiastes

Ecclesiastes 7

Ecclesiastes 7
King James Today

7:1 A good name is better than precious ointment; and the day of death than the day of one's birth.

2 It is better to go to the house of mourning, than to go to the house of feasting: for that is the end of all men; and the living will lay it to his heart.

3 Sorrow is better than laughter: for by the sadness of the countenance

Ecclesiastes 7

the heart is made better.

4 The heart of the wise is in the house of mourning; but the heart of fools is in the house of mirth.

5 It is better to hear the rebuke of the wise, than for a man to hear the song of fools.

6 For as the crackling of thorns

under a pot, so is the laughter of

the fool: this also is vanity.

7 Surely oppression makes a wise man

mad; and a gift destroys the heart.

8 Better is the end of a thing than the

beginning thereof: and the patient in

spirit is better than the proud in spirit.

9 Be not hasty in your spirit to be angry:

Ecclesiastes 7

for anger rests in the bosom of fools.

10 Say not you, What is the cause that the former days were better than these? for you do not inquire wisely concerning this.

11 Wisdom is good with an inheritance: and by it there is profit to them that see the sun.

12 For wisdom is a defense, and money is a defense: but the excellency of knowledge is, that wisdom gives life to them that have it.

13 Consider the work of God: for who can make that straight, which he has made crooked?

14 In the day of prosperity be joyful, but in the day of adversity

Ecclesiastes 7

consider: God also has set the one

over against the other, to the end that

man should find nothing after him.

15 All things have I seen in the days

of my vanity: there is a just man

that perishes in his righteousness,

and there is a wicked man that

prolongs his life in his wickedness.

16 Be not righteous over much;

neither make yourself over wise:

why should you destroy yourself?

17 Be not over much wicked,

neither be you foolish: why should

you die before your time?

18 It is good that you should take hold

of this; yea, also from this withdraw

not your hand: for he that fears

Ecclesiastes 7

God shall come forth of them all.

19 Wisdom strengthens the

wise more than ten mighty

men which are in the city.

20 For there is not a just man upon

earth, that does good, and sins not.

21 Also take no heed to all words

that are spoken; lest you hear

your servant curse you:

22 For oftentimes also your own heart knows that you yourself likewise have cursed others.

23 All this have I proved by wisdom: I said, I will be wise; but it was far from me.

24 That which is far off, and exceeding

Ecclesiastes 7

deep, who can find it out?

25 I applied my heart to know, and to search, and to seek out wisdom, and the reason of things, and to know the wickedness of folly, even of foolishness and madness:

26 And I find more bitter than death the woman, whose heart is snares and nets, and her hands as bands: whoso

pleases God shall escape from her;

but the sinner shall be taken by her.

27 Behold, this have I found, says

the preacher, counting one by

one, to find out the account:

28 Which yet my soul seeks, but I

find not: one man among a thousand

have I found; but a woman among

Ecclesiastes 7

all those have I not found.

29 Lo, this only have I found, that

God has made man upright; but they

have sought out many inventions.

Ecclesiastes 7

Doodles, Memory verse, Notes & Quotes

Ecclesiastes 8

Bible Verse Art 1) Pick a verse from the chapter. 2) Sketch in the words you want to bring attention to first—leaving space to add the rest of the verse above, below or around it. 3) Use your imagination to make the verse visually expressive.

Notes on Ecclesiastes

Ecclesiastes 8

Ecclesiastes 8
King James Today

8:1 Who is as the wise man? and who knows the interpretation of a thing? a man's wisdom makes his face to shine, and the boldness of his face shall be changed.

2 I counsel you to keep the king's commandment, and that in regard of the oath of God.

3 Be not hasty to go out of his sight:

Ecclesiastes 8

stand not in an evil thing; for he

does whatsoever pleases him.

4 Where the word of a king is,

there is power: and who may

say to him, What do you?

5 Whoso keeps the commandment shall

feel no evil thing: and a wise man's

heart discerns both time and judgment.

6 Because to every purpose there is time and judgment, therefore the misery of man is great upon him.

7 For he knows not that which shall be: for who can tell him when it shall be?

8 There is no man that has power over the spirit to retain the spirit; neither has he power in the day of death: and there is no discharge in

Ecclesiastes 8

that war; neither shall wickedness

deliver those that are given to it.

9 All this have I seen, and applied my

heart to every work that is done under

the sun: there is a time wherein one

man rules over another to his own hurt.

10 And so I saw the wicked buried,

who had come and gone from the

place of the holy, and they were

Ecclesiastes 8
King James Today

forgotten in the city where they

had so done: this is also vanity.

11 Because sentence against an

evil work is not executed speedily,

therefore the heart of the sons of

men is fully set in them to do evil.

12 Though a sinner do evil a

hundred times, and his days be

prolonged, yet surely I know that

Ecclesiastes 8

it shall be well with them that fear

God, which fear before him:

13 But it shall not be well with the

wicked, neither shall he prolong

his days, which are as a shadow;

because he fears not before God.

14 There is a vanity which is done

upon the earth; that there be just

men, to whom it happens according to

the work of the wicked; again, there

be wicked men, to whom it happens

according to the work of the righteous:

I said that this also is vanity.

15 Then I commended mirth, because

a man has no better thing under the

sun, than to eat, and to drink, and

to be merry: for that shall abide with

him of his labor the days of his life,

which God gives him under the sun.

Ecclesiastes 8

16 When I applied my heart to know wisdom, and to see the business that is done upon the earth: (for also there is that neither day nor night sees sleep with his eyes:)

17 Then I beheld all the work of God, that a man cannot find out the work that is done under the sun: because though a man labor to seek it out, yet he shall not find it; yea farther;

though a wise man think to know it,

yet shall he not be able to find it.

Ecclesiastes 8

Doodles, Memory verse, Notes & Quotes

Ecclesiastes 9

Bible Verse Art 1) Pick a verse from the chapter. 2) Sketch in the words you want to bring attention to first—leaving space to add the rest of the verse above, below or around it. 3) Use your imagination to make the verse visually expressive.

Notes on Ecclesiastes

Ecclesiastes 9

Ecclesiastes 9
King James Today

9:1 For all this I considered in my heart even to declare all this, that the righteous, and the wise, and their works, are in the hand of God: no man knows either love or hatred by all that is before them.

2 All things come alike to all: there is one event to the righteous, and to the wicked; to the good and to the clean, and to the unclean; to him that sacrifices, and to him that sacrifices not: as is

Ecclesiastes 9

the good, so is the sinner; and he that

swears, as he that fears an oath.

3 This is an evil among all things that

are done under the sun, that there is

one event to all: yea, also the heart

of the sons of men is full of evil, and

madness is in their heart while they live,

and after that they go to the dead.

4 For to him that is joined to all

the living there is hope: for a living

dog is better than a dead lion.

5 For the living know that they shall

die: but the dead know not any thing,

neither have they any more a reward;

for the memory of them is forgotten.

6 Also their love, and their hatred, and

their envy, is now perished; neither

have they any more a portion for ever

Ecclesiastes 9

in any thing that is done under the sun.

7 Go your way, eat your bread with joy, and drink your wine with a merry heart; for God now accepts your works.

8 Let your garments be always white; and let your head lack no ointment.

9 Live joyfully with the wife whom you love all the days of the life of your vanity,

Ecclesiastes 9
King James Today

which he has given you under the sun,

all the days of your vanity: for that is

your portion in this life, and in your

labor which you take under the sun.

10 Whatsoever your hand finds to do,

do it with your might; for there is no

work, nor device, nor knowledge, nor

wisdom, in the grave, where you go.

11 I returned, and saw under the

Ecclesiastes 9

sun, that the race is not to the swift,

nor the battle to the strong, neither

yet bread to the wise, nor yet riches

to men of understanding, nor yet

favor to men of skill; but time and

chance happens to them all.

12 For man also knows not his

time: as the fishes that are taken

in an evil net, and as the birds that

are caught in the snare; so are the

sons of men snared in an evil time,

when it falls suddenly upon them.

13 This wisdom have I seen also under

the sun, and it seemed great to me:

14 There was a little city, and few

men within it; and there came a great

king against it, and besieged it, and

built great bulwarks against it:

15 Now there was found in it a poor

Ecclesiastes 9

wise man, and he by his wisdom

delivered the city; yet no man

remembered that same poor man.

16 Then said I, Wisdom is better

than strength: nevertheless the

poor man's wisdom is despised,

and his words are not heard.

17 The words of wise men are

heard in quiet more than the cry

Ecclesiastes 9
King James Today

of him that rules among fools.

18 Wisdom is better than weapons of

war: but one sinner destroys much good.

❏ Copy KJT or My Way ❏ Definitions added ❏ Translation compared: _____

Ecclesiastes 9

Doodles, Memory verse, Notes & Quotes

Ecclesiastes 10

Bible Verse Art 1) Pick a verse from the chapter. 2) Sketch in the words you want to bring attention to first—leaving space to add the rest of the verse above, below or around it. 3) Use your imagination to make the verse visually expressive.

Notes on Ecclesiastes

Ecclesiastes 10

Ecclesiastes 10
King James Today

10:1 Dead flies cause the ointment of the apothecary to send forth a stinking savor: so does a little folly him that is in reputation for wisdom and honor.

2 A wise man's heart is at his right hand; but a fool's heart at his left.

3 Yea also, when he that is a fool walks

Ecclesiastes 10

by the way, his wisdom fails him, and

he says to every one that he is a fool.

4 If the spirit of the ruler rise up

against you, leave not your place; for

yielding pacifies great offences.

5 There is an evil which I have

seen under the sun, as an error

which proceeds from the ruler:

6 Folly is set in great dignity,

and the rich sit in low place.

7 I have seen servants upon

horses, and princes walking as

servants upon the earth.

8 He that digs a pit shall fall into

it; and whoso breaks a hedge,

a serpent shall bite him.

Ecclesiastes 10

9 Whoso removes stones shall be hurt therewith; and he that cleaves wood shall be endangered thereby.

10 If the iron be blunt, and he do not whet the edge, then must he put to more strength: but wisdom is profitable to direct.

11 Surely the serpent will bite without

enchantment; and a babbler is no better.

12 The words of a wise man's mouth are gracious; but the lips of a fool will swallow up himself.

13 The beginning of the words of his mouth is foolishness: and the end of his talk is mischievous madness.

14 A fool also is full of words: a man

Ecclesiastes 10

cannot tell what shall be; and what

shall be after him, who can tell him?

15 The labor of the foolish wearies

every one of them, because he

knows not how to go to the city.

16 Woe to you, O land, when

your king is a child, and your

princes eat in the morning!

Ecclesiastes 10
King James Today

17 Blessed are you, O land, when your king is the son of nobles, and your princes eat in due season, for strength, and not for drunkenness!

18 By much slothfulness the building decays; and through idleness of the hands the house drops through.

19 A feast is made for laughter, and wine makes merry: but

Ecclesiastes 10

money answers all things.

20 Curse not the king, no not in your thought; and curse not the rich in your bedchamber: for a bird of the air shall carry the voice, and that which has wings shall tell the matter.

Ecclesiastes 10

Doodles, Memory verse, Notes & Quotes

Ecclesiastes 11

Bible Verse Art 1) Pick a verse from the chapter. 2) Sketch in the words you want to bring attention to first—leaving space to add the rest of the verse above, below or around it. 3) Use your imagination to make the verse visually expressive.

Notes on Ecclesiastes

Ecclesiastes 11

Ecclesiastes 11
King James Today

11:1 Cast your bread upon the waters: for you shall find it after many days.

2 Give a portion to seven, and also to eight; for you know not what evil shall be upon the earth.

3 If the clouds be full of rain, they empty themselves upon the earth: and if the tree fall toward the south, or

Ecclesiastes 11

toward the north, in the place where

the tree falls, there it shall be.

4 He that observes the wind shall

not sow; and he that regards

the clouds shall not reap.

5 As you know not what is the way

of the spirit, nor how the bones

do grow in the womb of her that is

Ecclesiastes 11
King James Today

with child: even so you know not

the works of God who makes all.

6 In the morning sow your seed,

and in the evening withhold not your

hand: for you know not whether shall

prosper, either this or that, or whether

they both shall be alike good.

7 Truly the light is sweet, and a pleasant

Ecclesiastes 11

thing it is for the eyes to behold the sun:

8 But if a man live many years, and rejoice in them all; yet let him remember the days of darkness; for they shall be many. All that comes is vanity.

9 Rejoice, O young man, in your youth; and let your heart cheer you in the days of your youth, and walk in the ways

Ecclesiastes 11
King James Today

of your heart, and in the sight of your

eyes: but know you, that for all these

things God will bring you into judgment.

10 Therefore remove sorrow from your

heart, and put away evil from your flesh:

for childhood and youth are vanity.

Ecclesiastes 11

Doodles, Memory verse, Notes & Quotes

197

Ecclesiastes 12

Bible Verse Art 1) Pick a verse from the chapter. 2) Sketch in the words you want to bring attention to first—leaving space to add the rest of the verse above, below or around it. 3) Use your imagination to make the verse visually expressive.

Notes on Ecclesiastes

Ecclesiastes 12

Ecclesiastes 12
King James Today

12:1 Remember now your Creator

in the days of your youth,

while the evil days come not, nor

the years draw nigh, when you shall

say, I have no pleasure in them;

2 While the sun, or the light, or the

moon, or the stars, be not darkened,

nor the clouds return after the rain:

3 In the day when the keepers of the

Ecclesiastes 12

house shall tremble, and the strong men

shall bow themselves, and the grinders

cease because they are few, and those

that look out of the windows be darkened,

4 And the doors shall be shut in the

streets, when the sound of the grinding

is low, and he shall rise up at the

voice of the bird, and all the daughters

of music shall be brought low;

Ecclesiastes 12

5 Also when they shall be afraid of

that which is high, and fears shall be

in the way, and the almond tree shall

flourish, and the grasshopper shall be

a burden, and desire shall fail: because

man goes to his long home, and the

mourners go about the streets:

6 Or ever the silver cord be loosed,

or the golden bowl be broken, or the

pitcher be broken at the fountain, or

Ecclesiastes 12

the wheel broken at the cistern.

7 Then shall the dust return to

the earth as it was: and the spirit

shall return to God who gave it.

8 Vanity of vanities, says the

preacher; all is vanity.

9 And moreover, because the

preacher was wise, he still taught

the people knowledge; yea, he

gave good heed, and sought out,

and set in order many proverbs.

10 The preacher sought to find out

acceptable words: and that which was

written was upright, even words of truth.

11 The words of the wise are as

goads, and as nails fastened by

the masters of assemblies, which

Ecclesiastes 12

are given from one shepherd.

12 And further, by these, my son,

be admonished: of making many

books there is no end; and much

study is a weariness of the flesh.

13 Let us hear the conclusion

of the whole matter: Fear God,

and keep his commandments:

for this is the whole duty of man.

14 For God shall bring every work into judgment, with every secret thing, whether it be good, or whether it be evil.

Ecclesiastes 12

Doodles, Memory verse, Notes & Quotes

211

Help us help others (page 1 of 2)

Please share how you found this book helpful, or how God used it to affect you:

Help us help others (page 2 of 2)

Is there anything you would add to this type of book to make it better?

_____
_____
_____
_____

In what ways, or for what purposes did you use this book:

_____
_____
_____

Can you share a comment, complaint, idea, or suggestion?

_____
_____
_____

Tell us if you noticed an error in need of correction:

_____
_____
_____

❏ Please pray for the prayer request I have included in this mailing.
❏ Use the enclosed donation to continue reaching the incarcerated.

Optional: As an adult, I grant permission to publish, in any form, all or part of my comments *(this page front & back)* without compensation—allowing editing as needed.

X_____ _____ _____
Signature   Name Printed   Date

ECCLESIASTES-18 TITW 040919

Mail to: Renewing Lives, PO Box 4352, Diamond Bar, CA 91765-0352

CPSIA information can be obtained
at www.ICGtesting.com
Printed in the USA
BVHW011406160419
545683BV00010B/136/P